Lucy's Picture

Sara

Gillian

William

Katie

Sally

Daisy

Henry

Jonathan

Sam

Amelia

David

Timothy

Robert

Amanda

Belinda

Moss

Marcus

For Claire and Lucy
N.M.
For Gillian
A.A.

This edition is published by special arrangement with Dial
Books for Young Readers, a division of Penguin Books USA Inc.

Grateful acknowledgment is made to Dial Books for Young
Readers, a division of Penguin Books USA Inc. for permission
to reprint *Lucy's Picture* by Nicola Moon, illustrated by
Alex Ayliffe. Text copyright © 1994 by Nicola Moon;
illustrations copyright © 1994 by Alex Ayliffe.

Printed in the United States of America

ISBN 0-15-307311-X

1 2 3 4 5 6 7 8 9 10 026 99 98 97 96

Lucy's Picture

Nicola Moon

pictures by Alex Ayliffe

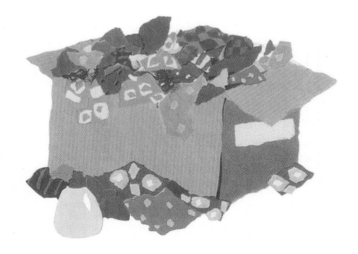

HARCOURT BRACE & COMPANY

Orlando Atlanta Austin Boston San Francisco Chicago Dallas New York
Toronto London

"My grandpa's coming to visit today," said Lucy. "How nice," said Mrs. Kelly. "Now, take a seat because we're all going to do some painting."

"Can I do a picture for Grandpa? asked Lucy.

"Of course you *may*," said Mrs. Kelly.

Lucy looked at the big sheet of white paper in front of her.

"Can't you think of what to paint, Lucy?" asked Mrs. Kelly.

"What would your grandpa like? Something nice and bright? Look at those lovely colors!"

Lucy looked at the red and the yellow and the sky-blue paints. "They're not right," she said. "May I use the glue? May I stick things on to make a picture?"

"You mean a collage? Of course! But you'll have to sit at another table. There's not enough room here."

Lucy took her paper to an empty table in the corner. She went and found a bottle of glue, some scissors, and the box of scraps.

Lucy loved Mrs. Kelly's box of scraps. She liked plunging her hands deep in the box and feeling with her eyes shut.

Lucy started her picture. She cut some soft green velvet into curvy mounds for hills, and stuck them on the paper. She made a lake out of blue shiny stuff, and put it in between the hills.

Then she found some flowery dress material.

"Grandpa has flowers like this in his garden," Lucy told Mrs. Kelly. Lucy cut around the flowers and stuck them in little clumps along the edge of the lake.

At recess Lucy was too busy to play. Instead she
collected twigs, leaves, and two small feathers. Then
she filled her empty juice cup
with sand from the sandbox.
At last it was time to go inside.

Now Lucy was even more excited about Grandpa's picture. She made him a tree out of the twigs and the leaves, and stuck the feathers on the end of a branch. Then she squeezed a long winding ribbon of glue over the hills, and sprinkled sand over the glue to make a path.

"My grandpa's got a dog," Lucy told Mrs. Kelly.
"She's called Honey because that's what color she is."
When Mrs. Kelly wasn't looking, Lucy trimmed
a piece of her own hair and glued it to a dog she had
made from a piece of paper.

Scrapbox

"That's lovely, Lucy," said Mrs. Kelly when it was storytime. She put Lucy's picture safely on the side to dry along with all the paintings.

Lucy couldn't wait to go home. She hadn't seen Grandpa in a long time.

Her mother was waiting as usual, but today there was someone with her.

"Grandpa!" cried Lucy. She nearly knocked him off his feet.

"I made you a picture, Grandpa. Look. . . ." Lucy grabbed her blind grandfather's hand and guided it over her picture. "These are hills, and here's the road. . . ."

Grandpa touched the picture carefully. "A tree. A bird. And what's this? It feels like your hair, Lucy."

"That's Honey!" said Lucy, smiling.

"How clever! And what a wonderful surprise. It's the best picture I've ever seen," said Grandpa.

Lucy

And hand in hand, Grandpa and Lucy and her mother walked home.

Sara

Gillian

William

Katie

Sally

Daisy

Henry

Jonathan

Sam

Amelia

David

Timothy

Robert

Amanda

Belinda

Moss

Marcus